Porcupine Quills to Needles

Tech from Nature

By Jennifer Colby

21st Century
Junior Library

Published in the United States of America by
Cherry Lake Publishing
Ann Arbor, Michigan
www.cherrylakepublishing.com

Reading Adviser: Marla Conn, MS, Ed., Literacy specialist, Read-Ability, Inc.
Content Adviser: Rachel Brown, MA, Sustainable Business

Photo Credits: © Thomas Gordon Roussell/Shutterstock.com, Cover, 1 [left]; © JPC-PROD/Shutterstock.com, Cover, 1 [right]; © tontantravel/Flickr, 4; © Awei/Shutterstock.com, 6; © KimSongsak/Shutterstock.com, 8; © Amanda Wayne/ Shutterstock.com, 10; © Badlands National Park/Lee McDowell, NPS, 12; © khiari raafet/Shutterstock.com, 14; © Steve Oehlenschlager/Shutterstock.com, 16; © tharathip/Shutterstock.com, 18; © karelnoppe/Shutterstock.com, 20

Library of Congress Cataloging-in-Publication Data

Names: Colby, Jennifer, 1971- author.
Title: Porcupine quills to needles / Jennifer Colby.
Description: Ann Arbor : Cherry Lake Publishing, [2019] | Series: Tech from nature | Audience: Grade 4 to 6. |
    Includes bibliographical references and index.
Identifiers: LCCN 2018035555| ISBN 9781534142961 (hardcover) | ISBN 9781534139527 (pbk.) |
    ISBN 9781534140721 (pdf) | ISBN 9781534141926 (hosted ebook)
Subjects: LCSH: Pins and needles—Design—Juvenile literature. | Porcupines—Juvenile literature. | Biomimicry—
    Juvenile literature.
Classification: LCC TS2301.P5 C65 2019 | DDC 646/.19—dc23
LC record available at https://lccn.loc.gov/2018035555

Cherry Lake Publishing would like to acknowledge the work of the Partnership for 21st Century Skills.
Please visit *www.p21.org* for more information.

Printed in the United States of America
Corporate Graphics

CONTENTS

Porcupines have over 30,000 quills.

On Defense

Have you ever seen a porcupine? If you do, stay away! They protect themselves with thousands of sharp **quills**.

Baby porcupines are born with soft quills.

Protective Purpose

Porcupines have quills to protect them against **predators**. The quills are a special type of hair. They are thick, stiff, and needle-like. Under a **microscope**, a porcupine quill looks very different. Each quill is covered with **barbs** close to its tip. The barbs face backward. This makes them very hard to pull out.

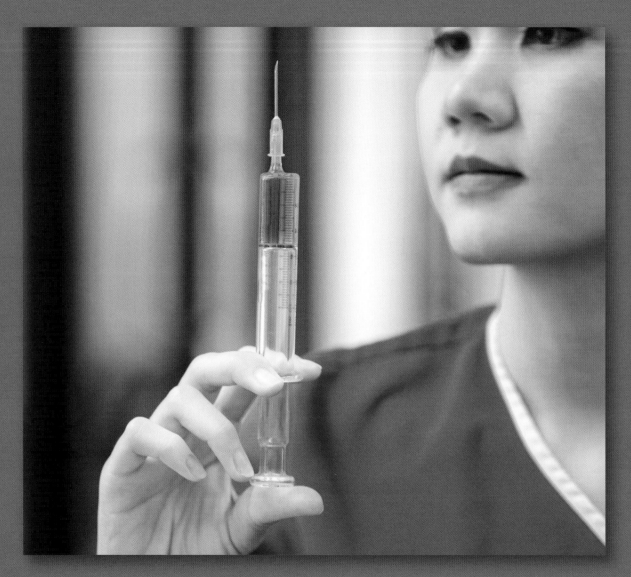

Medical needles have been around for thousands of years—
dating as far back as ancient Roman times!

Scientists study porcupine quills. They wondered if understanding quills could be helpful to the medical field.

Their research draws on the concept of **biomimicry**. Biomimicry is a rapidly growing scientific field of research. Let's take a closer look at what they are studying.

Make a Guess!

What type of animal do you think a porcupine is related to? Write down your guess. Give reasons why you think this. Read the next chapter. Was your guess close?

Porcupines are members of the rodent family.

Prickly Rodents

The word *porcupine* means "pig thorns." The porcupine's scientific name means "the animal with the irritating back." They are not animals that you want to get close to!

Porcupines are part of the rodent family. They are related to guinea pigs, mice, and squirrels. Porcupines are the second-largest rodent in North America. (The beaver is the largest.)

Some porcupines can climb trees.

The life span of a porcupine is 5 to 7 years. They can weigh over 40 pounds (18 kilograms) and can be about 3 feet (1 meter) tall. That's a big rodent!

Porcupines live in North and South America, Asia, Europe, and Africa. There are over two dozen species of porcupines. Some types of porcupines have needles that are over 1 foot (30.5 centimeters) long!

Some think that porcupines can "shoot" their quills. But this is not true. The quills are released when the porcupine swings its

Porcupines in the wild need to protect themselves.

tail or quickly backs into an animal. Animals that get too close to a porcupine can end up with quills stuck in their skin.

Medical **researchers** are studying how porcupine quills **penetrate** the skin. What if the **hypodermic needle** could be improved through the study of porcupine quills?

Look!

Ask an adult to help you do an internet search for porcupines. Compare porcupine species from around the world.

Curious dogs can get in trouble with porcupines.

Investigating Nature

Hypodermic needles are used mainly for two reasons: to give medicine and to remove fluid. When was the last time you got a shot? Chances are it was a little painful. People are generally afraid of needles because of that brief pain. In fact, the average 5-year-old has already received almost 50 shots. No wonder some people are afraid!

Have you ever donated blood or needed an **IV**? Needles used in these situations

Vaccinations, or medicines that are given through shots, keep us healthy.

have to stay in place for a long period of time. In order to keep the needle in place, doctors or nurses normally use tape. But that doesn't always work.

Because of this, a group of scientists are looking more closely at porcupine quills. Scientists noticed how the barbs on a porcupine's quill allow it to easily slide into the skin. They also noticed that the quills stay in place. They don't budge.

Scientists believe that a new type of hypodermic needle could be made. This new needle would penetrate the skin with less force. This would mean that getting a shot at the doctor's office would be less painful.

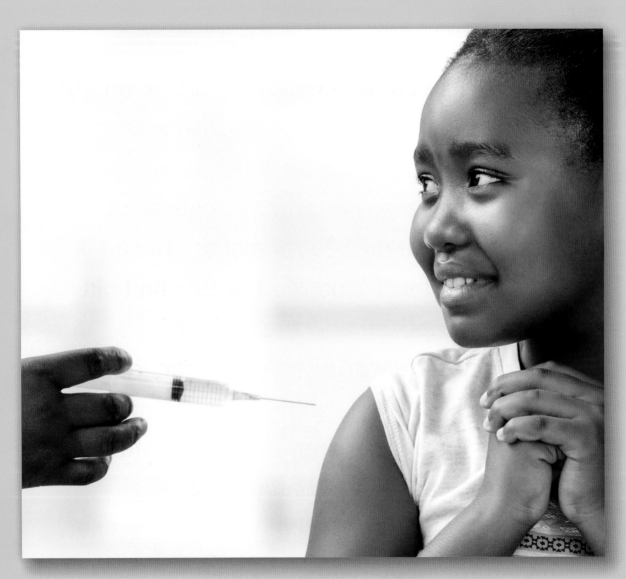

Getting a shot could be painless.

A needle that stays in place could be helpful for certain medical situations, like when donating blood.

To test their **theory**, they made a copy of a porcupine quill out of plastic. The quill-like needle easily entered the skin and did little damage.

Hopefully someday soon, we can thank porcupines for inspiring scientists to invent a less painful needle and a more useful device for medical professionals!

Ask Questions!

Ask a nurse or doctor what they think of this new invention!
Did they know the new needle was inspired by porcupines?
Are there other medical devices they think need improvement?

GLOSSARY

barbs (BAHRBZ) sharp points that stick out and backward from the point of a porcupine quill

biomimicry (bye-oh-MIM-ik-ree) copying plants and animals to build or improve something

hypodermic needle (hye-puh-DUR-mik NEED-uhl) a hollow needle that is used with a syringe to inject fluids into the body or remove fluids from it

IV (EYE-VEE) a device that is used to allow a fluid to flow, or drip, directly into a patient; IV stands for intravenous

microscope (MYE-kruh-skohp) a device used for producing a much larger view of very small objects so that they can be seen clearly

penetrate (PEN-ih-trayt) to go through or into something

predators (PRED-uh-turz) animals that live by killing and eating other animals

quills (KWILZ) hollow, sharp parts on the back of a porcupine

researchers (REE-surch-urz) people who do careful study to find and report new knowledge about something

theory (THEER-ee) an idea that is suggested or presented as possibly true but that is not known or proven to be true

FIND OUT MORE

BOOKS

Schwarz, Venessa Bellido. *Medical Technology Inspired by Nature.* Mendota Heights, MN: Focus Readers, 2018.

Sherman, Jill. *Porcupines.* Mankato, MN: Amicus Ink, 2019.

WEBSITES

National Geographic Kids—Porcupine
https://kids.nationalgeographic.com/animals/porcupine /#porcupine-mother-baby-log.jpg
Learn more about porcupines and then search this website for more information about other animals.

San Diego Zoo—Animals & Plants: Porcupine
http://animals.sandiegozoo.org/animals/porcupine
Learn more about porcupines and the other animals at the San Diego Zoo.

INDEX

ABOUT THE AUTHOR

Jennifer Colby is a school librarian in Ann Arbor, Michigan. She loves reading, traveling, and going to museums to learn about new things.